THE
GHOSTLY TALES
OF
SOUTHERN
CALIFORNIA

Published by Arcadia Children's Books
A Division of Arcadia Publishing
Charleston, SC
www.arcadiapublishing.com

Spooky America is a trademark of Arcadia Publishing, Inc.

First published 2023

All images used courtesy of Shutterstock.com; p. 6 kc_click/Shutterstock.com;
p. 34 Konstantin Yolshin/Shutterstock.com; p. 56 Steve Lagreca/Shutterstock.com;
p. 92 pablopicasso/Shutterstock.com; p. 102 lunamarina/Shutterstock.com.

Manufactured in the United States

ISBN 978-1-4671-9725-0

Library of Congress Control Number: 2023931838

THE
GHOSTLY TALES
OF
SOUTHERN CALIFORNIA

DAN ALLEVA

Adapted from *Haunted Southern California* by Brian Clune

arcadia®
CHILDREN'S BOOKS

NEVADA

CALIFORNIA

2 • BODFISH

6

SANTA MARIA

VENTURA 8

7

LOS ANGELES COUNTY

9 5

1 ★ LOS ANGELES

3

4

SAN DIEGO

UTAH

TABLE OF CONTENTS & MAP KEY

ARIZONA

Welcome to Spooky Southern California!

What comes to mind when you think of Southern California? Perhaps you envision one of its many beautiful beaches or ocean piers. Or maybe the famous celebrities of Hollywood, the movie capital of the world. Or it could be the legendary filmmaker Walt Disney and his influential amusement park, Disneyland. The park in Anaheim has been one of Southern

California's most treasured institutions for nearly seventy years.

While the ride at Disneyland suggests, "It's a small world, after all," there is so little that we know—or don't know—about what happens when darkness descends on the sunny shores of the Pacific Coast. When ghosts, ghouls, and lost souls wander the boulevards looking to give anyone who's *'California dreamin'* a nightmare they'll never forget.

Southern California feels like a place where the sun never disappears behind the clouds, and happiness is just around every corner. But don't be fooled! That facade is just as fragile as a Hollywood movie set. Because from San Diego to Hollywood and Santa Barbara to Death Valley, danger lurks in the shadows of Southern California, and there is plenty of haunting history to offer visitors who seek the supernatural.

This sun-kissed part of the country has its fair share of dark history, a history that many people don't know or don't want to know. And around every corner, you're likely to find spine-tingling tales of betrayals, murders, and tragedy that make it clear Southern California isn't *always* the place where dreams come true. Very often it's a land of lost and broken dreams turned into nightmares, where spirits and specters roam, looking for comfort, release, or revenge.

Wherever you go in Southern California, ghosts are waiting for you. Are you ready to meet them? Throw on your sunglasses, and let's begin our journey!

Hollywood Forever Cemetery

Where the Dead Remain Stars

There is no better place to begin our quest for ghosts in Southern California than a cemetery, especially one as famous as the Hollywood Forever Cemetery. Or should we say ... one as *restless*?

Hollywood Forever is known throughout the world because—you guessed it—so many famous people are buried here! In fact, this cemetery has so many movie stars, directors, writers, rock legends, and even *animal* celebrities buried within its grounds (like Terry, the little dog who played Toto in *The Wizard of Oz*), that you'd need at least a couple of days to visit all their gravesites.

That is . . . if the ghosts of Tinseltown don't find you FIRST.

Because at Hollywood Forever, the stars live on—even though they're dead! You might meet the ghost of legendary actress Judy Garland, who most famously played Dorothy in *The Wizard of Oz*. Or perhaps you'll run into in the spunky specter of Estelle Getty, who

played wise-cracking Sophia on the hit TV show, *The Golden Girls*. You might even hear the otherworldly echoes of celebrated voice actor Mel Blanc, who created voices for Looney Toons stars like Bugs Bunny, Daffy Duck, and Porky Pig, to name a few.

That's all folks!

Except—it's not. The list of famous people buried here goes on and on. There's legendary heartthrob and silent film star Rudolph Valentino, who died young at only thirty-one. There's Peter Lore, who acted alongside Humphrey Bogart in classic films like *Casablanca* and *The Maltese Falcon*. There's Hattie McDaniel, star of radio, film, and music, and notably the first African American to win an Academy Award for her role as Mammy in 1939's *Gone with the Wind*. And let's not forget Johnny Ramone, the leather jacket–wearing founding member of the 1970s punk rock band, The Ramones. (Was that a ghostly guitar solo I just heard? Or the wind, whispering through the trees?)

With so many big personalities sharing one eternal resting place (we're talking more than *eighty thousand* gravesites!), there's bound to be some spooky stuff going on. For years, people have reported strange lights, smells, whispers, and shadows while roaming the cemetery grounds. Some visitors have even noted the scent of perfume in the air, the sounds of sobbing, and drafts of icy cold.

Founded in 1899 and located on Hollywood's famed Santa Monica Boulevard, the cemetery sits right next to Paramount Studios. In fact, the renowned film studio was built on the back half of the cemetery grounds. There's even an entrance into Paramount Studios just a few feet from the cemetery, which is pretty convenient considering some of the movie stars and film directors buried here don't seem to know they're dead!

Night guards have reported seeing ghostly figures and spooky specters dressed in 1930s- and 40s-style clothing passing through the Lemon Grove gate—or even walking through the walls between the cemetery and the film studio! Could those be the spirits of legendary film stars and movie moguls heading to the set? As renowned actress Gloria Swanson (in the iconic role of Norma Desmond) said in the 1950 film, *Sunset Boulevard*, "Mr. DeMille, I'm ready for my close-up." (Fun fact: legendary American filmmaker, Cecil B. DeMille, is buried at Hollywood Forever.)

The cemetery offers ghost tours, but there's no need for a formal tour if you're excited to get ghost hunting. Visitors can simply purchase a map and seek out the spirits for themselves.

But be warned: if you're wandering around Hollywood Forever, chances are you just might wander into a dramatic scene!

One ghost who is said to haunt the cemetery is silent film star Virginia Rappe. It may be hard to imagine now, but the earliest films had no talking! They were "silent" films, as the technology was not available to match the sounds to the moving picture—a process known as *synchronization.* In fact, the music that accompanied these silent films was often performed live in the theater by an organist as the film played! (Can you imagine a *silent* Marvel Studios superhero movie? I think not!) Because there was no speaking in silent films, the actors needed to convey the entire story through their emotions, facial expressions, and costumes to be convincing on screen for the audience.

Virginia Rappe was a star of the silver screen in every sense. In 1917, she was named "Best Dressed Girl in Pictures." Unfortunately, Virginia met her untimely death on September 9, 1921, at the age of thirty. The official cause of death was a ruptured bladder and *peritonitis*—a condition where the organs in the abdomen become inflamed. It was a terrible loss for the world of cinema, and all of Hollywood mourned the passing of this bright young talent who was on the rise to fame.

Soon after Virginia's death, authorities came to believe that a friend of Virginia's—an actor named Roscoe "Fatty" Arbuckle—may have violently harmed her just days before when the pair had attended a party together, thus causing the injuries that led to her death. Suddenly, rumors began to swirl, and all of Hollywood was buzzing with questions.

The scandal became a national news

item. Arbuckle was accused of having caused Virginia's death and taken to trial three times. He denied the accusation and was acquitted (that means the jury found him not guilty), but went on to live the rest of his life as an outcast, ignored by the same Hollywood elite who had once adored him. Worse still, the world may never know what *truly* happened to Virginia on that fateful night in 1921.

She is buried in Section 8 of the Hollywood Forever Cemetery, and film fans and ghost hunters alike claim to feel her presence when visiting her grave. Some have said they hear screams bellowing up from the ground beneath her gravestone. Others have reported feeling a heartbeat pounding beneath the dirt where Virginia is (supposedly) resting in peace. It's claimed that you can actually put your hand to the earth and feel a *beating pulse* increasing in speed before it slowly and sadly fades away.

WHOA! That's enough to have *me* fading away—as in running for my life!

However, the most convincing proof that Virginia's ghost still haunts the grounds of the Hollywood Forever Cemetery is so terrifying, that if you visit, you may not want to linger for too long. If you *do*, you may very well come across Virginia herself, weeping softly. She's recognizable because of the 1920s style clothing she's wearing. Should you approach her, Virginia quickly retreats to her gravesite and then disappears. Whatever happened to her in life, she does *not* seem to want to talk about it in death.

However, not every story in this star-studded cemetery is surrounded by tragedy.

At the center of Hollywood Forever, there is a lake, and to its south, across Maple Avenue, is the Abbey of Psalms mausoleum. A mausoleum is a building used to store the remains of people who have died. Instead of being buried in the ground, they are placed in chambers behind walls, or in a vault under the floor. The word came from the name of an ancient king. Some of the stars who have been laid into eternal rest in the Abbey of Psalms include legendary director and silent film star Charlie Chaplin; actress Judy Garland, who starred as Dorothy in *The Wizard of Oz*; and that film's director, Victor Fleming, who also directed another famous film, *Gone With the Wind*.

Actor Clifton Webb might not have been as famous as his neighbors in the Abbey of Psalms, but he did have a respectable career in Hollywood. In 1950, he starred in the original version of *Cheaper by the Dozen*. (You may know the 2003 remake of this movie, which featured Steve Martin and Hillary Duff.)

Clifton Webb died in 1966 and was interned in the Abbey of Psalms. However, it seems that

Clifton has a hard time staying put in his vault! Many people have said they hear whispers coming from his regal tomb, while others have reported cold spots and peculiar lighting nearby.

Not frightening enough for you?

It's said you can often smell Webb's signature cologne throughout the Abbey, which typically means that Clifton is just over your shoulder. Turn and you may find him standing against his vault, sharply dressed in a suit and tie, plus a stylish hat of the period. Clifton doesn't usually say much, he just smiles and occasionally tips his hat. But stay alert, because just as soon as he appears, he *disappears* back into the shadows of the Abbey of Psalms. As it turns out, even character actors (that's someone who takes bit roles or plays eccentric characters in movies, just like Clifton Webb), never break their form, even in death.

In fact, the best actors often study their craft with an acting coach. So perhaps Clifton picked up some acting tips from his famous neighbor who rests just beside the Abbey of Psalms in the Cathedral Mausoleum. He was born in Southern Italy in 1895 as *Rodolfo Pietro Filiberto Raffaello Guglielmi di Valentina d'Antonguolla* (now that's a mouthful!). But to his many admirers around the world, he was known as Rudolph Valentino.

Rudolph was a handsome and charming actor adored by millions—you could almost think of him as the Brad Pitt or Chris Hemsworth of his time. His most famous role was in the epic war film, *The Four Horsemen of the Apocalypse*, which was so successful, it became the first film to earn one million dollars at the box office.

Sadly, Rudolph Valentino's fame—much like Virginia Rappe's—was short lived. In August of 1925, Rudolph became very ill with stomach ulcers. Believing he would make a miraculous recovery, Rudolph fought his sickness in secret. Alas, a happy ending was not meant to be. Rudolph died on August 23, 1925, after contracting *sepsis*—a very serious type of blood poisoning. He fell into a coma, then died a few hours later. At thirty-one years old, he was yet another star taken too soon.

Valentino's death caused hysteria around the world, and it's reported that more than eighty thousand fans attended his funeral. He was laid to rest in the Cathedral Mausoleum of the Hollywood Forever Cemetery. For the next thirty years, one of his dearest friends, a woman named Ditra Flame, would come to Rudolph's resting place. Wearing a black dress, she would lay a single red rose on his grave.

As is the case with most things in Hollywood, nothing remains a secret for very long, and soon people were desperate to learn more about this "Lady in Black" who was devoted to Rudolph.

Ms. Flame later explained that when she was a teenager, she was deathly ill. As a favor to her mother, Rudolph would visit her in the hospital, each time bringing a single red rose with him. Young Ditra was scared. She believed she was truly going to die, but Rudolph comforted the child as only the delightful thespian (that's another word for actor) could. He would sit by her bedside and assure Ditra, "You're not going to die at all. You are going to 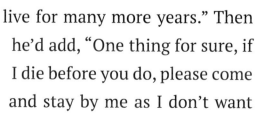 live for many more years." Then he'd add, "One thing for sure, if I die before you do, please come and stay by me as I don't want to be alone." Six years later, Rudolph died. But Ditra never forgot his kindness or what he had asked of her.

As the years passed, along with Ditra, imposters began to leave roses at Rudolph's grave. So many women in black would make their way to the mausoleum to leave a rose, it became impossible to tell who the original Lady in Black was.

Soon after, Ditra chose to stop leaving her roses—uncomfortable with all the attention, perhaps. And then she *really* stopped laying roses when she died in 1984. But since then, on the anniversary of Rudolph's death, there have been sightings of the "Lady in Black" at the Cathedral Mausoleum at Rudolph's vault. Is it simply another imposter? Could it be someone enamored with the sweet story of Rudolph and Ditra, who has taken up her duties? Or... is it *actually* the ghost of Ditra, forever fulfilling her promise to keep Rudolph company? Anything is possible, but it's nice to think it's the eternal spirit of Ditra, wouldn't you agree?

Today, you can visit the Hollywood Forever Cemetery, where there are many different attractions, including tours of the grounds and even an outdoor summer film festival, where thousands gather to watch dazzling film screenings under (and technically, *over*) the stars. Does it sound strange to you, watching a movie...while surrounded by movie star GHOSTS? Maybe it does seem a little odd. Either way, nothing should ever seem strange while visiting Hollywood. Least of all the customs of the living, because at the Hollywood Forever Cemetery, the dead are clearly still the toast of the town!

Built-to-Last Ghost Towns

Have you ever visited a *real* ghost town? Just a few hours' drive from the ghostly glitz and glamour of the Hollywood Forever Cemetery sits the Kern River Valley, home to many ghost towns. Nestled between the city of Bakersfield and Death Valley National Park, you'll find a whole slew of creeptastic towns sure to send shivers down your spine.

Once upon a time in the west, these

towns were bustling logging and mining communities, where prospectors came to seek their fortunes, and travelers stopped to rest (and play) on their way across the Sierras. During the gold rush era of the 1800s, places like Bodie, Calico, Darwin, and Willow Springs were in their heyday. But over time, drained of the gold, minerals, and other natural resources that once kept them alive and well, these towns fell into ruin. People moved on to places where they could make a better living. Thriving main streets became barren and desolate, with no inhabitants short of the occasional tumbleweed rolling through town.

Or should I say, tumbleweeds . . . and ghosts! *Plenty of 'em.*

After all, the Wild West wasn't called wild for nothing! There were crooked cowboys, gunslinging gangsters, rowdy outlaws, and infamous shootouts that not only left many dead, but some believe, left these towns very, *very* haunted,

Today, almost two centuries later, these places are major tourist attractions. Every year, curious ghost hunters flock to these eerie, abandoned towns, hoping for any trace of spirits or specters looking to make a cameo appearance. But a word to the wise: if you would like to visit Southern California's ghost towns, make your plans sooner rather than later. Unfortunately, many of these reminders of days gone by are being torn down and

replaced by roads, housing, and energy hubs. Still, there is one ghost town in the Kern River Valley that will very likely never disappear.

Even if it's not *technically* a genuine ghost town.

(But it sure looks like one.)

Welcome to Silver City Ghost Town: a historical museum in Bodfish, California, that was built to resemble a real-life ghost town— not only to give visitors a glimpse back into the area's rich and colorful history, but to help keep the spirit, shall we say, of Kern River Valley's ghost towns alive for generations to come. It's both a page out of history *and* a tribute to these long-since abandoned places.

Believe it or not, Silver City was originally supposed to be an amusement park.

In 1968, Dave and Arvilla Mills, who lived in the area, began to buy up many different ghost towns in the Kern River Valley—places like

Keysville, Claraville, old town Isabella, Whiskey Flats, Miracle, and South Fork—hoping to build their amusement park somewhere on one of the properties they'd acquire. That idea never came to be, but in nearby Bodfish, the Mills saw another opportunity. They decided they would use some buildings from the properties they had bought and open a "ghost town" of their own, hoping the place would attract tourists as well as those seeking out the supernatural.

When it opened, Silver City Ghost Town was a massive success. Located on the main road from Bakersfield to several other tourist destinations to the northeast, it was a logical place for people to stop along the way. Visitors wandered around the structures arranged to look like a ghost town. They asked Dave and Arvilla questions about the buildings and their history. Tourists left knowing a bit more about the area, and Dave and Arvilla felt like their dream was coming true. But, like the heyday of the *true* mining towns, the high times didn't last.

The rerouting of California Highway 178 in 1975 meant that road-trippers and other travelers now completely bypassed the small town of Bodfish—and Silver City Ghost Town along with it. The daily stream of cars, travelers, and adventurers, commonplace before the construction, came to a screeching halt. Sadly, three years after opening Silver City Ghost Town, Dave and Arvilla Mills closed its doors, turned out the lights, and built fences around the property they once dreamed would be a meeting point between the past, present, and future.

For over fifteen years, Silver City Ghost Town sat abandoned and undisturbed. Most people forgot about the attraction and, in a way—without a soul in sight—the museum started to feel like, well . . . a ghost town! Then, in 1988, a developer named J Paul Corlew decided to bring Silver City Ghost Town back to life. He purchased the property, restored the falling-apart town, and even built a gift shop and antique store to go with it.

In 1992, Silver City reopened its doors and has been alive and well ever since.

Know who else is alive and well?

ALL THE GHOSTS who call Silver City home.

You read that right. The "ghost town" pretending to be a ghost town . . . *is now an actual ghost town*!

From the ghostly cowboy seen strolling along the boardwalk, to the shadow spirits seen lurking around the gift shop, visitors to Silver City report *all kinds* of spooky things.

But where did all these spirits

come from? To our knowledge, no tragedies ever occurred in Dave and Arvilla's proud village—at least nothing that would indicate foul play or a need to return for unresolved business. The most likely scenario is that all that renovating, and all that *rebuilding*, caused some sleepy spirits who'd probably been there a looooooong time (like, since the actual gold rush) to WAKE UP! In most hauntings, it's widely understood that spirits can remain unannounced for eternity if not disturbed. But sudden changes—like a building renovation— can shake them from their other-worldly dimension and set them loose in ours.

Ghosts like Newt Walker, a gunslinger and gambler who was said to be the fastest draw who ever lived. He shot two men in self-defense but was charged with murder anyway. When the judge heard how two men had drawn pistols on Walker while his back was turned—and how fast Newt had drawn *his* pistol in return, shooting them both dead—the judge was so impressed he acquitted Newt on the spot, saving him from the gallows. Newt wasn't in the old Whiskey Flat Jail very long before he was freed, but some visitors claim he still makes an appearance every now and again. (Though, considering Newt barely escaped the noose once, one wonders why he'd want to return to jail ever again!)

Other ghosts who called Silver City home include an Indigenous man who sleeps (and reportedly snores) in the jailhouse. And Annie, who likes to photobomb tourists' pictures of the bait shop she used to own. We may never know exactly where all the spooky specters of Silver City came from, but one thing seems certain: how surprised Dave and Arvilla would be to know just how GHOSTLY their "ghost town" has become!

Sleeping Beauty's Castle at Disneyland

Welcome to Disneyland!

Did you know Disneyland is nicknamed the "Happiest Place on Earth?" It's no wonder why. From the very moment you walk through the park's iconic gates in Anaheim, California, you enter a world of magic, fun, and pure imagination. A world full of thrilling rides, mesmerizing attractions, culinary delights, and beloved characters from your favorite movies, cartoons, fairytales, and more. A world where dreams come true.

But did you ALSO know the happiest place on earth . . . is one of the most *haunted*?

That's right, Disneyland is full of ghosts! And if you dare to look beyond the park's sparkling exterior, you'll find enough spooky stories to scare you silly.

Take the Haunted Mansion, for example. Here, guests climb into "Doom Buggies" for a frightfully fun journey through an eerie estate full of phantom spirits and ghostly ghouls. Where apparitions dance the waltz and spunky spirits regale you with song. But ghost hunters and cast members alike know the truth: those are all just part of the attraction. And the Haunted Mansion's *real* ghost is a little boy who—when he was alive— loved this ride more than anything.

Most of the time, the boy is seen trying to catch the ghosts that dance around the banquet hall, or peeking at guests from behind the gravestones in the cemetery section. He seems to be having as much fun on the ride in death as he did in life. Though, others have said they have seen the boy quietly crying near the exit, as if he's wondering where his mother is and why she left him here.

According to the story, the boy's mother knew this was her son's favorite ride. Which is why she decided to sprinkle his ashes there after he passed away. It might sound creepy, but this is a regular occurrence at Disney properties. For years, people have been coming from all over the world to spread their loved ones' ashes around the parks, ensuring they'll be happy for all eternity.

(Talk about a happily ever *after-life!*)

In fact, ash spreading has become so common, that cast members are hired to look out for this very thing! There are also security cameras everywhere, but somehow, guests still manage to sneak ashes in. With so many peoples' ashes having been scattered at Disneyland over the years, there's a good chance that when you're strolling down Main Street, U.S.A., you're strolling among the living . . . *and* the dead.

Some claim to have seen a different ghostly boy on another favorite attraction: Pirates of the Caribbean. Apparently, he's often spotted sitting alone in one of the empty boats, or occasionally, in an empty row in an otherwise full boat. He doesn't react when the boat starts to move, nor does he seem afraid. He simply stares straight ahead, as if lost in a dream, and always vanishes as the boat comes to a stop at the end of the ride.

Another well-known Disneyland ghost is the "woman in white." Usually seen after dark, she walks slowly down Main Street in a long, white gown. Though nobody knows for sure who she was in life, in *death* people often describe her as a force for good who helps guide lost children back to their families.

It makes sense that most of the ghosts at Disneyland are happy haunts. Still, even at the happiest place on earth, not all stories can have happy endings. While Disneyland goes to great lengths to protect its guests and ensure a magical (and above all *safe*) time, accidents can happen. And the truth is, with so many people passing through the park each year, it's inevitable that some of them might just end up staying ... forever.

In the summer of 1966, a teenage boy named Thomas Cleveland made a fatal mistake. He wanted to celebrate Grad Night at Disneyland with his friends, but he did not have a ticket. So, he decided to sneak in. Though he managed to scale the sixteen-foot fence and cross the Monorail track without being seen, it wasn't long before a guard spotted him. Spooked, Thomas took off. He sprinted back the same way he came and darted onto the tracks. Tragically, seconds later, the Monorail sped around a corner and struck the young man. He died instantly. To this day, always late at night, some monorail riders report seeing a ghostly teenage boy running ahead on the monorail tracks, forever trying to outrun the train.

A handful of years later, in 1973, two brothers decided they didn't want to leave Tom Sawyer's Island at closing time. They managed to hide themselves well enough and stayed out of sight in an off-limits section of the

island. But after a while, with nothing to do—and no rides to ride—they found themselves getting bored. Because the boats had stopped running, they decided to swim back to the main park.

Big mistake.

The older brother, Bogden, could swim just fine. But his ten-year-old brother, Dorian, couldn't. Just before midnight, they started across the Rivers of America, with Dorian perched on Bogden's back. But halfway across, the two began to struggle. Nobody heard their cries for help and they both slipped under the water. Somehow, Dorian was able to make it back to shore. But Bogden never did. He wasn't found until the following morning. To this day, some say they have seen ghostly ripples on the water's surface in that very spot. Could it be Bogden's restless spirit, trying to swim back to shore?

Another tragedy struck the park in 1984, when a woman named Dolly Young was killed on the Matterhorn bobsled rollercoaster. Though cast members always take extreme precaution when it comes to safety, Dolly's seatbelt somehow came unbuckled and she was thrown from the ride and struck and killed by an oncoming bobsled. To this day, cast members claim Dolly's spirit haunts the area of the track where she died, known as "Dolly's Dip."

But the most *famous* ghost who has been seen around Disneyland is none other than the man who created it all—Walt Disney, himself.

Walt used to entertain guests in a room known as the Walt Disney Gallery. It was just above the entrance to the Pirates of the Caribbean ride. Many people who have taken a tour of the gallery claim to have seen Walt. They say he is simply standing there with a smile on his face, perhaps just happy knowing that, even long after his death, people are still enjoying the park he created. And seeing Walt smile has made *them* smile.

However, Walt's spirit has been spotted all over Disneyland. Apparently, the wishing well near Sleeping Beauty's Castle is a favorite haunt of his, and he's also been seen strolling down Main Street. Perhaps the most convincing story about Walt's everlasting presence at the park was told by a cast member: One night, while working in an office that Walt had once used, she suddenly felt a presence, as if someone was standing behind her. The cast member wasn't scared or alarmed, as she knew that whoever, or *whatever*, was with her meant her no harm. She went about her work, and later, as she left, she heard a whisper behind her. *I'm still here*, the voice said.

It seems even from the great beyond, Disney's spirit continues to watch over his beloved park.

If the ghost of Walt Disney truly does reside within the walls and gates of the masterpiece he created, it's undoubtedly because such joy is too pure—and too rare—of a thing to leave behind.

I guess that's the thing about the happiest place on earth: some people never want to leave.

Elfin Forest

Eerie Elfin Forest

If you stop for a moment within the breathtaking woods of the Elfin Forest in San Diego County, you'll likely hear a songbird chirping, perched on one of the many trees that cover the seven-hundred-acre site. Mist often swirls around the twisted trees, gnarly bushes, hanging moss, and bright foliage. In the Elfin Forest, it's easy to imagine you're in a place where fantasy is real. In fact, that's a bit how the forest got its name. You see, the whimsical glades and glens of Elfin Forest reminded one of its former owners of places like Rivendell and the Shire, home to the hobbits and elves

that make up the magic of J.R.R. Tolkien's *The Hobbit* and *Lord of the Rings* book series. Although Tolkien never visited these woods, it's not hard to imagine the late author taking in Elfin Forest's enchanting landscape and agreeing with the comparisons to his own land of fantasy.

But what would a forest be without traces of the supernatural rustling through its leaves? Just as Tolkien's world wasn't safe from ghouls and goblins (really nasty ones, too), neither is Elfin Forest. At least, that is what many people say. Stories of Elfin forests sometimes mix fact and fiction, and most are believed to be urban legends. But whether they are true or not, they still make people pause before stepping foot into the forest.

Take Questhaven Road, for example. Between sixteen and twenty car crashes happen in this area every year, and authorities cannot explain why there are so many accidents along this stretch of road. Of course, one answer could be drivers are suddenly startled and distracted by the presence of a specter known as the White Witch.

Most people believe the White Witch was originally a local townswoman. One night, the woman, her husband, and their young son were set upon by bandits. They killed her husband and son, but the woman managed to escape. Although she mourned the loss of her family, more than anything, she was angry. She vowed to seek revenge on the men who took her family from her. It's said she went into the local villages and sought to the learn the "magic" of the nomadic and Indigenous peoples living in the area. As the story goes, she left the village soon after, supposedly able to cast a powerful mix of magic and spells. She was never seen again.

Well, never seen *alive* again.

However, something very curious happened after the woman left town. People began to see a woman in white along the trails of Elfin Forest. The phantom has no feet, and she hovers above the ground, mist circling around her as she silently moves through the forest. People say they do not sense any harm from the spirit, nor do they feel she is angry or vengeful. Why she chooses to haunt this section of woods around Questhaven Road is uncertain. But if you see her, it's probably best to give her plenty of space. After all, it is a forest, and there should be room for everybody, wouldn't you agree? Though, drivers beware.

Interestingly enough, the White Witch is

not the *only* witch that haunts these enchanted woods. Plenty of people have had many chance encounters with another paranormal presence known as the Black Witch.

According to legend, the Black Witch believes she is the guardian of Elfin Forest, and one simple glance into her eyes brings madness and death to any unfortunate soul who encounters her. It's said that long ago, she was one of the nomadic people the nearby settlers cast out of Elfin Forest—but not without the Black Witch casting a curse upon the whole town.

The land of Elfin Forest once belonged to the Kumeyaay/Diegueño Peoples of North America. According to legend, when the nomads came with their magic, the departed children of the Diegueño people rose from the dead! The white settlers reportedly began seeing ghost children in their town squares, and would hear them playing long into the night.

Angered by the nomadic people and their spells, the white settlers cast them violently from Elfin Forest, killing many along the way. The Black Witch is said to have been a high priestess within the nomadic caravan, and on her way out of the forest, she cursed the forest and the townspeople forever. To complete her curse, she killed herself along the forest's edge to assure her ritual would work.

From that day forward, a mysterious woman cloaked in black, often on horseback, rides through the forest, marking any who cross her path for certain death. It's said that once you've been marked by the Black Witch of Elfin Forest, she will not rest until the deed is complete. All she needs to do is take one look into your eyes to send you into an unraveling spiral of madness and horror! She can end life in an instant, so whatever you do, *run* for your life if you see her. Those who claim to have seen the Black Witch never forget her, leaving shattered minds filled with terror.

But the dangers of Elfin Forest don't end there. There are also reports of strange lights floating among the trees, whispers coming from the thick brush, and an eerie wind that disappears as quickly as it arrives. Some claim

to have seen a stylish Englishman wandering in the forest. He wears a top hat, carries a walking stick, and swings a lantern as he makes his way along the paths. Who he is, where he's come from, and where he's going remain a mystery.

If you do visit Elfin Forest, you may have the good (or bad?) fortune of spotting one of the ghastly ghosts that haunt this part of Southern California. So be sure to keep your wits about you. And remember . . . if you see a woman dressed in black, *don't* look her in the eye!

Aztec Hotel

The Dazzling Apparitions of the Aztec Hotel

Along historic Route 66 in Monrovia, California—in the foothills of the San Gabriel Valley—sits a famous hotel with a mysterious past. Once a roaring twenties hot spot, the hotel is ornately designed and looks a little bit like an ancient temple.

But don't try to check in. Because the Aztec Hotel no longer *operates* as a hotel.

At least ... not for the living.

(If you're a ghost, though, you're welcome any time you like.)

Back in the day, the Aztec Hotel was a popular hangout for movie stars, mobsters, and bootleggers. (A bootlegger is someone who sells illegal goods. Nowadays, that's most likely pirated movies and music. During the Prohibition era in the 1920s, it was alcohol.)

Even though it was illegal to buy and sell alcohol during America's Prohibition Era (which lasted from 1920 until 1933), bootleggers delivered a steady supply of it to people, clubs, and restaurants who wanted it. And the Aztec Hotel was one of those places. It was a playground for everyone, so it's no wonder that the ghosts who remain there still like a party every now and again!

One ghost that still haunts the hotel goes by the name of Razzle Dazzle. Not much is known about Razzle Dazzle, other than she has dark hair styled in a finger-wave (a glamorous vintage hairstyle where the hair is set with waves or curls), and carries a long cigarette holder, fashionable in the 1920s. There are stories that Razzle may have met her demise after being struck by another guest in the hotel, a man she had an argument with at a certain point in the evening. No one can say for sure what happened to Ms. Dazzle, other than she often haunts Room 120, which may have been the room she was staying in. Guests who have stayed in that room have awoken to find her standing at the foot of their bed, or worse yet, lying down next to them!

What would you do if you woke up next to a ghost? I don't know about you, but I wouldn't know what to do first: run or scream! I guess it's a good thing the Aztec isn't currently taking any guests. But still, note to self: scratch Room 120 off the list.

Willie, who manages the hotel's restaurant, the Mayan Bar and Grill (where the living are *perfectly* welcome to enjoy a delicious meal), has seen more ghosts than he would care to count. When Willie first joined the staff at the Mayan, he had a strange occurrence. As he walked through the VIP room, he heard a whistle. Willie didn't think much about it since there wasn't anyone else nearby. But just in case, he stopped and took a look around, confirming there was no one there. Or so Willie thought. As he continued his walk through the VIP room, he heard the whistling again.

Now that is not normal, thought Willie.

Later, when he came back through the VIP room, someone, or something, came up beside Willie and whistled into his ear!

Willie demanded that whoever was whistling should cut it out. And then, just like that, the whistling stopped. At least for Willie. Soon after, Willie's coworkers began to hear the whistling as well, though no one could ever figure out where it was coming from.

Willie also tells the tale of a black-haired man he spotted sitting in a chair in the hotel lobby. Willie assumed this man, who was wearing a green shirt and black pants, was waiting for the bar manager. When Willie told the bar manager that there was someone waiting for her in the lobby, she gave him a funny look. She wasn't expecting anyone. So, Willie and the bar manager made their way back to the lobby, only to find the chair empty. The bar manager casually told Willie it must have been one of the hotel ghosts. Ever since then, Willie has laid a tablecloth over the chair in hopes it will keep ghosts from taking a seat there.

The source of the Aztec Hotel's paranormal activity may have a logical explanation. (That is, logical if you believe in ghosts!) During Prohibition, the Aztec had an underground speakeasy—a place where patrons could party and enjoy alcoholic drinks out of sight of the police. In fact, at one time, there were at least two tunnels underground leading out from the Aztec Hotel so guests could escape in case there was a police raid.

Today, two rooms still exist from that speakeasy, and one of them is called the Green Room. It is rumored to contain a vortex—or a passageway—to another dimension, allowing spirits of all kinds to walk in and out of our world at their leisure. Willie says he's never experienced any kind of paranormal activity there, but many ghost hunters and psychics *have*, and they claim it is the heart of the hotel's spooky happenings.

Because of its unique architecture and design, the Aztec Hotel was designated a National Historic Landmark in 1978 and is listed on the National Register of Historic Places. It's still not open for hotel guests, but that might be okay. After all, you might not want to encounter the ghosts who refuse to check out!

Spirits and Suspense at the Santa Maria Inn

There must be something about hotels that makes them such an attraction for ghosts and other unexplained phenomenon. Maybe the ghosts enjoy the steady stream of guests who go in and out of the hotel. After all, there will *always* be new people to scare at a hotel.

The ghosts of the Santa Maria Inn in Santa Maria, California, certainly seem to enjoy spooking all the new people they meet. Though some ghosts may prefer to keep to themselves, the ghosts of the Santa Maria Inn are *skilled* at making themselves known.

Built in 1917 by a man named Frank McCoy, the Santa Maria Inn was one of the most modern and luxurious hotels of its day. Because it was so grand, a lot of very important and high-profile people wanted to stay there. People like Charlie Chaplin, the world-famous movie star and director. Mary Pickford, the glamorous star of stage and screen. Bob Hope, the beloved comedian, actor, singer, and dancer. And remember Rudolph Valentino, one of the stars buried at the Hollywood Forever Cemetery? Even he stayed at the Santa Maria.

Little did any of them know, this legendary hotel would someday be considered one of the most haunted places in Southern California!

(Not to mention, *their* ghosts would be doing some of the haunting!)

Handsome Rudolph, for starters, is said to haunt Room 221, the room where he stayed whenever he visited the Santa Maria Inn. But he must not know he's a ghost—or that this is no longer his room—because he's often heard pounding forcefully on the door, a fact that proves *frightfully* annoying to the guests staying there! The rapping usually begins at night, just as the guests are falling asleep. When they open the door, there's no one there, of course. And despite calls and complaints to the front desk, the pounding resumes as soon as the guests snuggle back under the covers. Ultimately, the inn's staff can only shrug. It seems even ghosts can throw celebrity temper tantrums!

Want to hear something else extremely creepy about Room 221?

Hotel staff say that when the room is unoccupied, an imprint of a body can be seen in the made bed, as if someone is lying there. But even creepier still, Rudolph has been seen standing by the bed, looming over an unsuspecting dozing dreamer. I wonder if he learned that trick from Razzle Dazzle over at the Aztec Hotel?

But while Rudolph may have been a leading man during his short career in Hollywood, he's

only a supporting character when it comes to the Santa Maria Inn. The star of the show here is undoubtedly a man known to all as the Captain.

The Captain began making regular appearances at the Santa Maria Inn not long after it opened, though not much is known about this mysterious character. Some say his affairs of the heart got him into trouble, and he was murdered by a jealous lover, which is why he still lingers around the hotel. The Captain can be seen at any time, day or night, but for reasons unknown, he seems to gravitate toward Room 210. That said, the Captain is a bit of a wanderer, and he can turn up anywhere.

Once, while the inn was being renovated, a couple staying on the first floor complained of hearing loud noises. It sounded like someone was stomping heavily up and down the staircases and slamming doors. Because of the renovations, the couple thought it might have been a worker. But why would they make such a racket that late at night? When the couple inquired, of course, no work had been scheduled for the prior evening. That's when the couple learned about the Captain. The inn's staff believed he was just having a laugh with the couple and meant no harm. Though, I'm sure they didn't find it funny at all!

The Santa Maria's strange and spooky happenings don't end there. Over the years, guests have reported lights suddenly strobing, and eerie shadows following them down the

hallways. Visitors often hear the sound of a piano playing softly and sweetly. In most cases, this would be soothing to the ear. But the fact that *no one is actually playing the piano* is definitely not soothing.

Oh, and don't forget the strange footprints in the garden, and the sounds of cellar doors slamming (even when nobody's remotely close to the cellar). As you can see, nearly every corner of the Santa Maria Inn has been a site of odd and mysterious activity.

But wait! There's more! Like the guest who went to a vending machine, hungry for a late-night snack. But instead of a snack, they got nothing but fear and fright! The guest hadn't put any money into the vending machine, and yet—somehow—it was working on its own. (Actually, free snacks don't sound so bad.) Then again, the same guest claimed that a fork and knife appeared from out of nowhere, as if held by invisible hands.

Hmm.

On second thought, perhaps best not to eat from the vending machines at the Santa Maria.

Just in case.

The Santa Maria Inn gets good reviews on Trip Advisor, the website that rates hotels and

tourist attractions. And apparently, the ghosts get good reviews as well, minus all that banging on the door. (I'm looking at *you*, Rudolph.) So, if you're in the area, the hotel might be worth a stop. The staff of the Santa Maria Inn—and its illustrious ghosts—are sure to make your stay a memorable one!

The Camarillo Hospital of Horrors

Driving down the Pacific Coast Highway toward Ventura County—your parents blasting "Hotel California" on the radio, and the ocean sparkling as far as the eye can see—it's hard to imagine *anything* but good vibes, good music, and a sky full of sunshine.

And yet...just a few miles inland...the vibes were once VERY dark indeed.

There aren't many people alive today who can still recall its "era of terror," but for those rare few, the name *Camarillo State Hospital* likely triggers memories of the most *unthinkable* torture that happened inside these otherwise unassuming walls. It's a place that sends shivers up—*and* down—the spines of those who remember its horrors. Today, it's known as the Channel Islands State University, and it's frankly so haunted, and *so* jam-packed with restless souls, it's a wonder students get any work done at all.

From 1936 until 1997, the state hospital in Camarillo housed thousands of patients, many of whom were struggling with mental illness issues. After a time, the hospital grew so large and housed so many patients, it became a small town in its own right. There was a neighborhood of houses for the staff, as well as a farm and dairy that supplied the hospital—and the town of Camarillo—with produce and milk. The hospital was self-sustaining and remote, so people didn't question what was going on there. Little did they know that evil was masquerading as science, with patients forced to undergo terrible procedures supposedly meant to "cure" them.

Procedures like lobotomies, which involve the removal of or alteration to a part of the brain, and electroshock therapy, a treatment that involves shocking a person's brain with an electric current. (See? I told you it was scary.) Some patients were left all alone in a pitch-black room for long periods of time as another form of "treatment."

Make no mistake about it, Camarillo State Hospital represented a low point for mental health treatment in the United States. Fortunately, doctors and scientists later embraced kindness and humanity, not pain and suffering, as crucial keys to healing. But there's no doubt the cruelty that took place at Camarillo State Hospital has led to the myriads of hauntings within these *incredibly* spooky walls.

The area of the campus once used as the children's ward is perhaps the most haunted of all. Many have reported hearing the faraway voices and eerie laughter of children at play. When the hospital was still open, the children were often allowed to run around in a fenced-in area that served as a playground. While no fence or playground exists today, spectral children can be seen spinning on merry-go-rounds and riding up and down on teeter-totters, without any idea they are dead.

Apparitions have been seen in windows

of the university. Sometimes, they're gazing at a particular person, but often they're just staring into nowhere, as if their minds have been unlocked and tampered with in the most monstrous of ways. However, there are times when there is a look of cold-blooded murder in their eyes. If you do catch sight of one of these phantom children, whatever you do, do *not* get in a staring contest.

Inside the building, ghosts have been known to roll items down hallways. Some visitors are overcome by panic when they step inside certain rooms, only to feel relief upon stepping back out. It's as if the pain and agony of the former patients still lingers inside these rooms. Their cries for mercy can be heard practically everywhere. It's a horrible reminder of what took place at Camarillo State Hospital.

For years, ghost hunters have flocked to the Channel Islands University campus to search for specters and capture EVPs. (EVP stands for electronic voice phenomenon, sounds that are thought to be spirit voices.) During one such visit, a ghost—not caring for the tone of one of the ghost hunters—called him quite a nasty word, which they were able to pick up on the recording devices. Let's just say that ghost hunter kept his opinions to himself after that encounter!

If you're brave enough to venture down the dirt lane a little ways down the road from the university, you'll come to a place known today as the "Scary Dairy." Supposedly, many ghosts have decided to make their home in the barn—including one who is said to call out the names of people as they walk by, trying to lure them into the barn. So if you hear your name being called, keep walking! And you might also want to hold your nose, because this section of campus is known for its rotting stench of spoiled cheese and milk. Some even compare the scent to that of a "wet cow." YUCK!

The good news is, the Camarillo State Hospital shut its doors in 1997. Many of the original buildings are now on the National Register of Historic Places, meaning they have been spared from being torn down. So today, the students at Channel Islands State University have a place to live and learn— and the ghosts of former patients have a place to haunt. Let's just hope the students who decided to study here know what they got themselves into, attending one of most haunted universities in the world!

The Majestic/
Ventura Theater

When you go to the movies with your family or friends, you probably know what to expect. Plush seats, *check*. Buttery popcorn, *double check*. Sticky floors from the soda your annoying little brother just spilled, *triple check*.

(Sigh.)

And course, most fun of all, is the movie itself!

But did you know that every time you go to

the movies, there's a good chance the person sitting by themselves a few rows over isn't actually a person . . . but a GHOST?

Because guess what: people aren't the only ones who love going to the movies— ghosts love them, too! (Especially *High S-ghoul Musical*. I'm told that's a favorite.)

And where better to visit a haunted movie theater than Southern California, the movie capital of the world? From the Wilshire Theater to the Beverly to the world-famous Grauman's Chinese Theatre (known today as the TCL Chinese Theatre), this part of California has no shortage of notable—and notably *spooky*—cinemas.

But by far, the most haunted of them all is the old Ventura Theater, now known as The Majestic.

The Ventura Theater opened on August 16, 1928, to a sold-out crowd. In those days, there weren't epic summer blockbusters or animated features like you're probably used to seeing at the movies, on Netflix, or even Disney+. There was no Marvel Universe, no *Star Wars*, no *Minions*, and definitely no *Harry Potter*. Instead, the Ventura Theater's first audience enjoyed a mixed bag of entertainment. There were a few news clips as well as a few film serials—today, we call them "shorts"—and even a feature film called *Excess Baggage*. The

night closed with a vaudeville act and dancing troupe, but to be honest, it didn't really matter what the evening's entertainment was. Motion pictures were so new that filmgoers were just happy to see whatever films they could! Plus, the Ventura Theater's glorious construction only added to the excitement. All night long, audience members marveled at its beauty. Entering the theatre was like walking into a different world.

(Perhaps the ghosts in the room felt the same?)

Three stories tall, the Ventura Theater owed much of its look to the influence of Spanish architecture, which of course had been brought by the Spanish when they'd colonized the area. Intricate shapes and exquisite patterns were built into every corner of the Ventura Theater, making it one of the most elaborate movie theaters in the world. In fact, some even said it rivaled the opulent palaces of Europe. The lobby even had a life-size model of a seventeenth century Spanish ship! It was lined with antique furniture, chairs, and sofas so guests could relax in the lobby—probably during an intermission or a break in the performance, which was common of movies at that time. From the sky blue and sunburst ceiling décor, to the grand iron handrails that lead to beautiful balconies, the Ventura Theater was an incredible site to see.

Today, not much is left of that original structure. But there are *plenty* of spirits on hand from those days, so check your seat before you sit down—it may already be taken.

The most infamous ghost at the now Majestic Theater is truly a bizarre specter. It's simply known to many as the "What" ghost.

WAIT—a ghost named "What"? you might be asking yourself, and for good reason. "Why" is probably a better question to ask.

Well, the answer is pretty simple. This ghost, for reasons that are totally a mystery to everyone, likes to walk up behind people and utter the word "*what*" into their ears. No one knows why the ghost whispers "*what*" to moviegoers. Some believe this spirit is sensitive about space, and he may not be happy about having crowds of people in his home.

"What," as the staff have come to refer to this wandering spirit (who turns up wherever he pleases), is harmless. Though his one-word question might sound a bit rude, people who work at the Majestic say a simple apology usually sends him on his way.

Another harmless apparition who frequents the halls of the Majestic Theater is Eddie, who serves as a guardian of this historic location. Eddie is generally said to be easygoing. However, if he witnesses unruly patrons acting disrespectfully toward his staff, Eddie is known to act—and act *fast*. He has reportedly tripped and pushed people, making it clear that those patrons should either behave, or *get out*. So always be on your best behavior in any theater, but especially the Majestic, as Eddie doesn't play around!

Undoubtedly, the most disturbing ghost at The Majestic is also the saddest. During tours of the theater, people have seen a young girl dressed in white dancing across the stage. It's not her graceful dancing that catches their attention—it's the fact that she doesn't have a head! No one knows for sure who this young girl is, but there are several theories.

One is that she was a student at Ventura High School in the 1930s. During a rehearsal for a show in the theater, some girls were messing around and one of them fell into what is now the control room. The poor girl either broke her neck or was (gulp) decapitated by the sharp metal stairway. Another story goes that during rehearsal for the prom, a sheet of glass suspended from the ceiling suddenly came loose and sliced off her head. Luckily, no matter how she lost her head, the fact that she doesn't HAVE one doesn't seem to take away from her exquisite dance skills.

As for the rest of the ghosts of the Majestic Theater, they love nothing more than to play around. Spirits have been seen moving levels and twisting knobs on the soundboards, forming as mists in the fading spotlights, and moving chairs in the orchestra.

Whatever their reason for being there, ghosts *abound* at The Majestic Theater, and if you visit, there's a good chance you'll encounter one. But remember, before you hand the attendant your jacket, make sure they're one of the *living* attendees!

Universal Studios

We end our journey through Southern California back where we began, in Hollywood. You may be surprised to know this, but Disneyland isn't the only major theme park in Southern California. (Fun fact: it's not the only *haunted* theme park, either.)

Welcome to Universal Studios, the only amusement park where you can see your favorite movie stars, whether they are dead or alive, walking through the backlot!

To tell the spooky story of Universal Studios, we need to travel back in time. Originally, Universal Studios began as a film production company on the East Coast. The studio produced some of the most iconic and classic monster and horror movies, such as *Dracula*, *The Mummy*, *Frankenstein*, *The Creature from the Black Lagoon*, and *The Invisible Man*. These films were so gripping, they still wow audiences today.

The man originally in charge of Universal Studios was an innovator named Carl Laemmle. He was a man with big ideas and the will to make them reality. His original movie studio was located in New Jersey, but he knew he needed a bigger space to expand his successful operation. (Not to mention, he was also competing with inventor and businessman, Thomas Edison, who was just down the road and also working on films at the time.) With the movie business beginning to boom, Laemmle

moved his operations to Hollywood. He bought a 230-acre converted farm in the San Fernando Valley that would soon house one of the most famous movie studios in the world.

Universal Studios opened at this location in 1915. After many successful years in business, and with the technology that soon became available, Universal began inviting fans into their studio, which was ultimately converted into a theme park. People of all ages enjoyed attractions like the "Studio Backlot" tour.

Little did studio executives know, they had also welcomed *ghosts* onto the lot!

In fact, it seems that ghosts started taking up residence at the studio just as soon as it opened. Frank Stites was a stunt pilot who Carl Laemmle had hired to perform for guests at the studio's grand opening. But to everyone's surprise (and horror), Stites's plane got into trouble during his performance. Rather than waiting for the plane to crash, Stites jumped from the plane and was killed. That should have been the end of Frank Stites, but it wasn't. Ever since the tragic accident—and it's been more than a century—people have seen a man dressed in a vintage pilot uniform and a leather helmet wandering around, presumably so that he and his amazing stunts won't be forgotten.

So many famous actors that have graced the lots of Universal Studios can be seen in spirit form nowadays, including actor Lon Chaney, who played the Phantom in *The Phantom of the Opera*. He used to hang around sound stage 28. He would often be seen peering over the shoulders of cameramen preparing to shoot, or strolling along the catwalks. Sound stage 28 was one of the older stages at Universal, and it was torn down to make way for rides in the amusement park. But that obviously hasn't deterred Lon Chaney. For decades, visitors and film crews alike have spotted him enjoying the rides in the same area where sound stage 28 used to be. He must be having a grand time—because he never wants to leave!

Mr. Chaney is not the only specter said to walk the grounds of Universal Studios. So do the ghosts of Lucille Ball, who rose to fame as the lovable Lucy character on the hit show *I Love Lucy*, and the great master of suspense, director Alfred Hitchcock, who gave us such classic horror-thrillers as *Psycho* and *The Birds*. It's said Steven Spielberg (the director of movies like *Jaws*, *E.T.*, *Indiana Jones*, and *Jurassic Park*) once used the same office on the lot that Hitchcock had. As the story goes, Hitchcock monitored Spielberg's work so closely that Spielberg insisted on finding a new office to work out of.

(Alfred's spirit, in the meantime, continues to haunt Universal Studios to this day. Apparently, he liked hanging around at the Shrek attraction and was none too pleased when it closed down.)

Next to Jurassic Park: The Ride, stands a gift shop dedicated to this famous dinosaur movie franchise. A little girl about nine years old is often seen wandering around inside the gift shop. One day, worried she might be lost, a gift shop clerk approached the child to ask if she needed help. But as the clerk came closer, the girl simply shook her head *no*, and vanished.

She didn't stay gone for long, though.

Soon after, another clerk reported seeing an eerie mist moving around the store. As the mist lingered, the clerk heard a giggle, and suddenly merchandise started flying off the shelves and onto the floor. Pretty dramatic—which makes sense since she's at Universal Studios.

Other specters around the park are known for playing tricks on passing guests. Cast members report strange happenings in the area where they clock in and out—apparently the work of a mischievous specter boy. Lights flicker and doors slam, even when they're all alone.

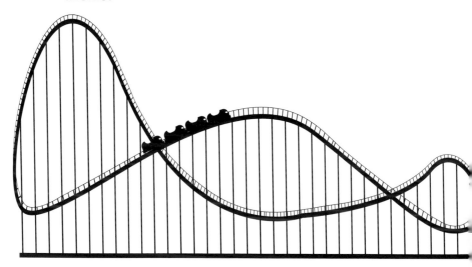

Or . . . are they?

The good news is, like Disneyland, most of the haunts here are happy. Just remember, if you get scared on one of the rides, be sure the hand you grab beside you belongs to a member of the living!

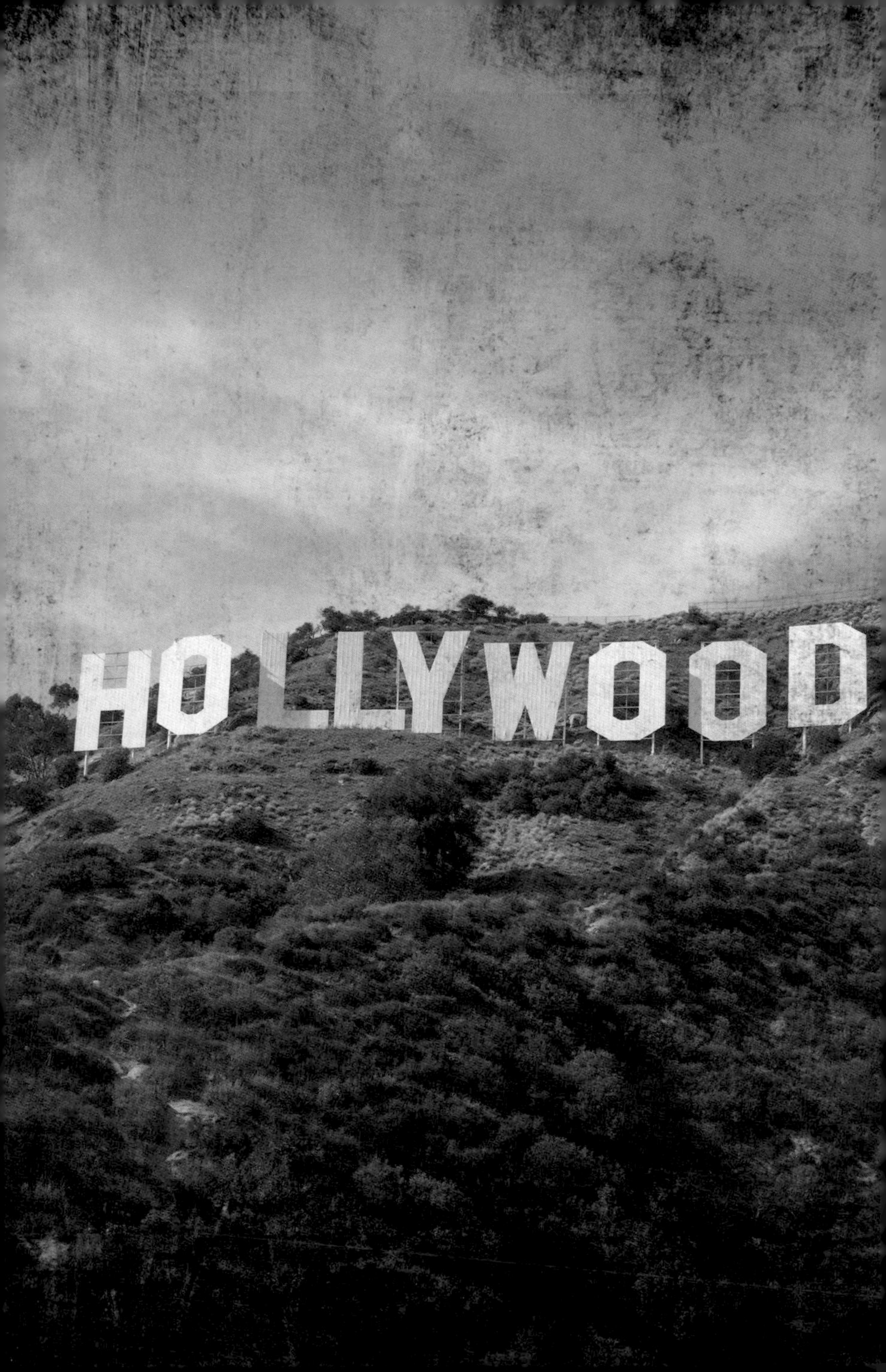
HOLLYWOOD

A Ghostly Goodbye

Southern California attracts tourists from all over the world. They come to splash in the waves and soak up the sun at the beautiful beaches. They take tours of movie studios, learning how movies are made, and hope to catch sight of their favorite stars. They delight in swooping and soaring on rides at the "Happiest Place on Earth." Whatever reason people come to this idyllic spot, most of them never realize there is an entire other world lurking just out of sight. One that is *much* darker and more chilling than the one they have come to visit.

Most folks who come to the sunny shores of Southern California won't see the ghostly crew still working at the movie studio, even though they punched out decades ago. They won't spot the budding movie star still trying to get her big break, even though the curtain has come down on her life. They don't experience the knocking at their door and the echoing footsteps at their hotel, where some guests

refuse to check out. And they won't encounter the man who wants to make sure that—even in death—his "Disney Dream" is still bringing joy to tourists from around the world.

But now that *you* know who—or what—to look for, keep your eyes and ears open. You may be lucky enough to catch a glimpse of the ghostly side of Southern California. Either way, you can truly take comfort in the fact that here, you're never alone.

Dan Alleva is an author, editor, and journalist from Brooklyn, New York. You can read his daily news stories from the world of music online at Metal Injection (metalinjection.net), and find some of his truly hilarious *Mad Libs* titles in your favorite local bookstore. When not writing, Dan can be found rooting on his beloved Manchester United, or at the beach with his wife and daughter, and their sweet little doggie, Georgia. You can learn more at www.danalleva.com.

Check out some of the other *Spooky America* titles available now!

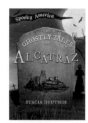

Spooky America was adapted from the creeptastic *Haunted America* series for adults. *Haunted America* explores historical haunts in cities and regions across America. Here's more from the original *Haunted Southern California* author Brian Clune: